First
Facts®

Spiders

Jumping Spiders

by Joanne Mattern

Consultant:
Pedro Barbosa, PhD
Department of Entomology
University of Maryland, College Park

CAPSTONE PRESS
a capstone imprint

First Facts is published by Capstone Press,
151 Good Counsel Drive, P.O. Box 669, Mankato, Minnesota 56002.
www.capstonepub.com

 Books published by Capstone Press are manufactured with paper
containing at least 10 percent post-consumer waste.

Library of Congress Cataloging-in-Publication Data
Mattern, Joanne, 1963–
  Jumping spiders / by Joanne Mattern.
     p. cm.—(First facts. Spiders)
  Includes bibliographical references and index.
  Summary: "A brief introduction to jumping spiders, including their habitat, food,
and life cycle"—Provided by publisher.
  ISBN 978-1-4296-4524-9 (library binding)
  1. Jumping spiders—Juvenile literature. I. Title. II. Series.
  QL458.42.S24M38 2011
  595.4'4—dc22
                                   2010002256

Editorial Credits
Lori Shores, editor; Veronica Correia, designer; Eric Manske, production specialist

Photo Credits
Dwight R. Kuhn, 8, 16, 19
© Gerry Lemmo, 11
iStockphoto/James Benet, 20
James P. Rowan, 21
Pete Carmichael, 7, 13, 15
Shutterstock/Dark Raptor, 4; orionmystery@flickr, 1; Steve Bower, 5; sunsetman, cover

Essential content terms are **bold** and are defined at the bottom of the page
where they first appear.

Printed in the United States of America in North Mankato, Minnesota.
012011   006038VMI

Table of Contents

Jumping spiders are less than 1 inch (2.5 centimeters) long. But these spiders can do something amazing. They can jump more than 40 times the length of their bodies. If you could do that, you could jump over your house!

Spider Fact!

Jumping spiders are some of the fastest running spiders.

Hairy Bodies

Jumping spiders have thick, hairy bodies. Like all spiders, these **arachnids** have two main body parts and eight legs. Some jumping spiders are bright red. Others have striped legs.

Spider Fact!

A jumping spider has four eyes on the front of its head. Four more eyes are on the sides and top of its head.

arachnid—an animal with four pairs of legs and no backbone, wings, or antennae

abdomen

cephalothorax

Spider Fact!

Jumping spiders hang on to draglines with tiny leg hairs.

dragline

Staying Safe

To stay safe, jumping spiders use **draglines** when they jump. The spider sticks a strand of **silk** to a leaf or a rock. Then it jumps. If the spider misses its target, it can swing down safely on the silk.

dragline—a silk string that prevents a spider from falling
silk—a string made by spiders

Where the Spiders Are

More than 4,000 kinds of jumping spiders live all over the world. About 300 kinds of jumping spiders live in North America.

where jumping spiders live

Jumping spiders have been found on Mount Everest, the tallest mountain in the world.

Most jumping spiders live in hot, tropical areas. Others make their homes in forests, deserts, and even mountains. Jumping spiders can also be found in people's homes.

Hunting Skills

A jumping spider hunts for **prey** during the day. The spider creeps up on small insects. When it gets close, the spider pounces on its prey.

prey—an animal hunted by another animal for food

Time to Eat

A jumping spider has two long, sharp **fangs**. When the spider bites prey, **venom** flows through the fangs. The venom quickly kills the prey.

The jumping spider squirts juices into the prey's body to turn it into liquid. Then the spider drinks up its meal.

fang—a long, pointed toothlike mouthpart
venom—a harmful liquid produced by some animals

fangs

eggs

egg sac

Family Time

Male and female jumping spiders join together to produce young. Then the female lays more than 100 eggs. She puts them in a silk **egg sac** under a rock or leaf. The mother spider guards the eggs.

Spider Fact!

Some jumping spiders make small tentlike nests to hide their egg sacs.

egg sac—a small pouch made of silk that holds spider eggs

Growing Up

Spiderlings stay in the egg sac after they hatch. The mother spider brings food to her young. After a few weeks, the spiderlings leave the sac. They find homes and hunt on their own.

Spider Fact!

Jumping spiders seem to be curious. They will jump up on a human hand instead of running away.

spiderling—a young spider

Life Cycle of a Jumping Spider

Newborn

Spiderlings hatch out of their eggs after a few weeks.

young jumping spiders

Young

Young spiders shed their outer skeletons several times as they grow.

Adult

Adult jumping spiders live about two years.

A Leg Up

Jumping spiders have eight strong legs for leaping. Each of their legs has seven **joints**. The joints allow the legs to bend so the spiders can jump.

joint—a place where two leg parts are fitted together

Amazing but True!

Jumping spiders have the best eyesight of all spiders. These spiders can see up to 8 inches (20 cm) away. That's pretty far for such a small spider! Scientists think jumping spiders can even see colors.

Glossary

arachnid (uh-RACK-nid)—an animal with four pairs of legs and no backbone, wings, or antennae

dragline (DRAG-line)—a silk string that prevents a spider from falling

egg sac (EG SAK)—a small pouch made of silk that holds spider eggs

fang (FANG)—a long, pointed toothlike mouthpart

joint (JOYNT)—a place where two leg parts are fitted together

prey (PRAY)—an animal hunted by another animal for food

silk (SILK)—a string made by spiders

spiderling (SPYE-dur-ling)—a young spider

venom (VEN-uhm)—a harmful liquid produced by some animals

Read More

Bishop, Nic. *Spiders.* New York: Scholastic Nonfiction, 2007.

Goldish, Meish. *Jumping Spiders.* No Backbone! New York: Bearport Publishing, 2009.

Hartley, Karen, Chris Macro, and Philip Taylor. *Spider.* Bug Books. Chicago: Heinemann Library, 2008.

Internet Sites

FactHound offers a safe, fun way to find Internet sites related to this book. All of the sites on FactHound have been researched by our staff.

Here's all you do:

Visit *www.facthound.com*

Type in this code: 9781429645249

Index